Rose About Thirteen Pedals

Nellya Yurukov&Iliyan Yurukov

ISBN 10:1499572352
ISBN-13:978-1499572353

DEDICATION

We are grateful to the American poet, award winning author "Fire and Ice' journalist and interviewer on BlogTalkRadio Dianna Bellerose and her family.

Thanks poetess Fira Zavyalova for active participation in the Gallery (our grandmother and mother).

Thanks to the head Sait "Poets for Israel" Adam Dobrzyński Israel.

Thanks for the support of scientists, journalists Eastern Europe and America.

Nellya Yurukov & Iliyan Yurukov

ACKNOWLEDGMENTS

Shalom Aleichem is the third volume!

Tutorial!

Rose about thirteen pedals!

Philosophical and psychophysical sketch image in art In the research process of change issues

Climatic and geographical conditions as well as changes in the structure of the crustal structure, there was a great migration of people in connection with what has changed, worldview, ways of development of foreign lands and cultures before the formation of Sciences.

There is a change of psychophysical and mental human development - the emergence of new forms of economic activity and the level of development of material production. What led to the change of the environment, ways of thinking? There is a need to improve skills and knowledge in order to send them to succeeding generations.

The mathematician, astrologer, mythological thinking, rudiments of writing (signs, symbols, icons), appears right-handedness and improved the anterior lobe of the brain.

We used monographs from known experts.

"The history of medicine" - (John Tiner).

"The history of Psychology"- (David Hothersall).

"A History of Philosophy"- (Phrederick Copleston).

"Philosophy of Art"- (Noel Carroll).

"My Stroke of Insight"- (Jill Taylor).

1) The Future!

Why all people?

The idea on the future disturbs?

Why we where we were?

And seats suddenly these have emerged.

Why we remember the childhood?

Meteoric shower and tenderness of mums.

Why agitates?

Time in the world? Who, except for us?

In fact biologists repeat.

The decay bypasses precisely you.

It is a way to new system.

Perfection in the Universe.

And circle circulation.

Minerals and bacteria and so.

Electrolyte is so live.

Memory who's that protects.

Why drops at Ocean?

Those will return together with us.

Water is interesting to all.

How many that remembers always?

If to atoms all to merge.

Through millions years what to repeat?

Is that can be way of reincarnations?

Concepts and obstacles.

Denying the law.

Dialectics, it is combined.

The world as stairs abrupt.

With each step ennobles.

It the law of grandfathers, fathers and the son.

To repeat all have a good day.

And the pray will save up.

The sign from the God will send us.

Therefore the Lord is so   lovely.

Torah to us friends has handed over.

Gallery!

(2) What are the common symptoms?

What are the common symptoms?

As soon as he is Lord?

Than he moved, hold?

And no doubt about it at all?

Relaxation is important.

What force it is given? Circuit long always.

How to get to you?

In the ancient world.

Qi and Dao refund?

Oil Lawrence on the road.

And further, that same are you?

As for us water is important.

Many secrets are storing it.

How to raise us from the ocean?

Secrecy all and without deception?

See if you can guess them secrets.

Are you agreeing on defense cooperation?

Um, Lemuroids, and other.

Mathematician you are intact.

Experience ancestors and fathers.

Than Japan is strong?

That the experience

What kind of experience gained?

Okinawa, cocoon is there.

Save descendants, us.

Gallery!

3) How many times you taught us!

As soon as she graduated from our idea.

Communication with yourself.

Suggested that in fact the wave.

Speed of light it is given.

That of course is boredom. And chemically is real.

Electromagnetic. How is it?

Who have the idea that you can radiate.

Your brain is clearly takes it.

Each has a recipient.

Takes all that there is.

Who is talented, those who do not.

Protects it from ills?

Vertically with God we are.

Push beams. Because, who is to blame?

Guess that this is a fact.

Brain will record all and all.

 Protected or not?

Why not all prayers? Will be heard or seen.

Important moral and motive.

Accommodating enough force?

Whether all Gents you forgave him?

So we look forward to seeing prayers mix.

The same shall we ask.

Lord, realized it all, introduction.

How many times I forgave him.

How many times you've taught.

How many times again unto thee.

It is important to know what motive.

That is not honest it will return.

That crime would be very costly.

If the thief, is being punished.

That consciousness, desecrated?

Gallery!

(4) Vitamins!

Vegetables and fruits.

 In the middle of winter.

Vitamin deficiencies.

We have escaped. Disease prevention.

 All tastes there are. And the title is very much.

Not all installations. Oranges, tangerines. Juice pour out.

Children love these fruits. Grow burly. They are all against infection.

At each step, people should know about this.

I'll help them. Vitamins reveal any.

And of any size. And Israel is proud with the wealth.

Children are bright for example.

Fira Town, Public Relations Director

(5) Diamond with rhinestones!

Swiss milk. Chocolate, taste it for connoisseur.

From the Swiss product.

Pharmacologically, and antioxidants are here.

And what are there medicines?

We buy them so often. Alps for tourists.

The funicular, running quietly in their deerskin moccasins.

As well as the meadows?

The paintings all of it. "Red Cross" to the international.

The whelp: Symbol and noble.

Innovations, patents, certificates that look.

The beauty of the prophet you are.

Here elegance of stone.

And optical friends.

And fluorescent signs.

Those on the road are very holy.

Swiss Cheese for the hungry.

Here are the runaway will soon emerge.

Air net, sports a large.

A legend here with the soul.

Gallery!

6) 36 Prophets children!

There are milestones on the planet.

The link is visible only in the light of the.

Earthly, poets and of course children.

And who are they? As you understand.

Who? Christians had to justify their divisions? Leads.

Why is nitrogen? So liquid?

Same reason why a prominent?

The same myth we guess?

As fate we defend?

The same knowledge to understand?

Why Osiris again? And Abkhaz journalists mask or become?

Why don't scientist's ceremonies have become to explore?

Philosophy the beginning, famous Falez with beautiful views that would be the matrimony?

In the upbringing he messenger. He was a scientist and an example.

Eternal Compass he invented.

He predicted such a harvest.

Their beaux capital. Children he had envisaged.

Kant planet firmly knew. The moral imperative loitered.

For cardiac arrest two, he miracle knew. He sky with the Bible taught.

In "flight over cavity". The Kizi became its main architect. (See also "ship it". As philosophy understands.

Now mat huge barrage.

Why don't scientist's ceremonies have become to explore?

Philosophy, the beginning, famous Falez with beautiful views, which would be the matrimony?

In the upbringing, he is messenger.

He was a scientist and an example.

Eternal Compass invented it.

He predicted such a harvest. What is the level, the emotion?

At the start there was who?

Those who reason people handed over?

What in the future will be the plan?

Our modeled on has created.

Gallery!

7) Egyptians!

Why is the pyramid?

From the people, the eyes are hidden?

Why is the same, and rays?

Do not pass through sands?

Where is the sand? From what he has saved.

That, the secrecy? Where is the sand?

This is quartz, he has saved? From what is a desert?

Or not the thoughtless?

That same in the chamber there is a?

The space, shower honor.

With his clients?

This knowledge deep.

For the plane?

And why children gender me?

Why is it so maintained? But others have been burned?

Can gene from them, in his mind.

And clowning those.

Can this be repeated cycle?

We will repeat the fantasy

Gallery!

8) Tesla!

Tesla Serbia, you son.

8 University citizens.

Electricity a gloomy desert I traversed.

That same you have opened.

Electricity, the king.

Such a supernatural cognition.

He has experienced both worlds.

Example reason has become.

Station furious in candescence.

The things you are moving.

Presents manganese silicide - compound in love with her.

Knew and did, a lot. Navigation stronghold. "Tesla" and is now live.

Aircraft takes. It protects people.

Lightning strikes you are the king and the glory.

Gently guarded   secrecy. Ophir vertical take off.

Phone and thought. How many plans, who will find it.

Century dream thy handmaid, I donated you are suitable.

Technology has begun.

Gallery!

9) Spain! Picture,

"Prado", I toured with.

 What goodness storefronts.

For that, I love poetic skills.

Spain is not easy. Columbus entirely encased in Alaska.

Almost America has opened up.

Karim, Rashid there in pink colors.

The hotel's facade and for us.

Velasquez, Frida you DÃ©cor, as milo.

Here comes a bright but it wasn't so easy.

And Goya passion. there with his disciples.

And Picasso, always for peace. You fond" dove of peace".

The emblem was impressed with all of us.

A globe is a girl.

And it cast a shadow over the runs do not be anxious about tomorrow.

Those who had not imitated?

Who are the Muslim? So does not stand?

The materials or props is not difficult.

The center of balance it is.

Gallery!

10) Karate!

A very fine delicate art print on canvas --- agniart.ru.

You're invisible, and let. You with nature like merged.

You are glowing in the minds.

Black Belt, white time zone.

This is you as one-hundred-and-Americas.

Here we bearing it is important. Philosophy replay.

Here east and did not die in vain.

Force valued, so it is clear.

But it indeed and clever.

Protects as always.

Live, live and all to gather.

Senior must be respected.

Babies of all detest. The wife always shivers.

You do not twist the great adventure film.

Star it is you, you know. Strand fragile you hanging.

And rapidly is just flowing. Guard you country.

Karate for the love.

 Gallery!

11) Architecture!

Century steel architecture.

Very wise fixtures. Unusual glass.

The entire building is an easy one.

If we Americans. A lot of love, logs, dancing.

If Greece, so what?

And Bulgaria Veliko Tarnovo is given.

If you're an Israeli?

It is garden fascinated.

And yet we love pile. If puddles it under us.

And another asphalt with us. This tiles effects.

It is very clean and attractive.

Is geometric, very mil?

We Love palm trees, we always loved it.

Adorn the city. Fruit the first diet.

And 120 us for this. The east, so they're shish.

Turned the captain.

Gallery!

12) Providentially!

5 It has been civilization.

How many explosions and stagnation?

Come from the ground.

A piece a small Moon. Changed tilt axis.

Have to see on another. Red, yellow nerve moaned.

Atlantis recalled. It may have been in the Savanna is unsurpassed?

Who are the assumed, and yes the survived?

Peace for them is so changed.

Fear over them all owned. Information is away.

Intuition is strong. Children are all the same, navy.

Back to technology. We are drilling, crew send.

And underline its land.

Gallery!

13) Vercingetorig!

Vercingetorig son exhausted, leader Keletila!

The Family information site that are for the people.

And that the myths? Who leads?

You princes oak and was able to.

And how many people had endured the roads?

The Family information site, Gauls tribes. Irish, Britov, you are a star.

Top tier elite, and it is important.

And secret knowledge of you is full.

And the nature and doctors. And the livings are long gone.

The trees, hands shook their heads.

There currents, with whom they are related to?

Shower trees, ancestors, you.

As had been the road characteristics.

The stars the way they found it. Galaxies are **asleep**,

You are twins. Where is your language?

Is it drifted into the consciousness?

You poets, and priests. ogamicheski scars.

For that "you field? For that you France Mila.

And where was the ancestral home?

Did you love gently you horse?

Chief Arvernov, your strategist.

Diplomat, and knew that he could.

I initiated wars, lives lost. Leader for Gauls everlasting has become. Christianity, traditional healers and Barda.

And knowledge, your tracks.

Even in Turkmenistan, their minds.

Would like to know, what are they?

We are all in the same Hwang Sok. How fair is thy love?

It is not spoken about you.

Where to you is our interest?

But you are in Turkmenistan.

There is the same Aksum, the sons.

Uzbek athletes there are courageous.

There revenues knowledge is determined.

For that for your roads and us.

For those same objects was Oleg?

And the sunrises, the century?

Gallery!

14)Nevena Peleva, my sister!

Plovdiv, Plovdiv, Filipopol.

As he loved his lord the king.

How many have been here dreams.

Delicate dreams and expectations.

How many songs and love. Air is clean, all in the front.

Parks, grandmother and you. It is those, not grumblers.

You Filipopol peace, is clear.

You are bright and mig and not microcredit | Outsourcing | Insurance | Personals. My childhood there has passed.

It Komativo sla. You Maritzei, entire fortress.

You riasen positions before heading north.

Fair thy prophet. Del Quirinale was fighting.

How many sights and events. It is very bright and great lakes.

The old Plovdiv, your museum.

I questioned how many spark plugs.

It is architecture the choir. Buildings are bright here, and rooms.

And hotels are very important.

And award-winning sports is different. City teenager, doctors.

Tobacco Control, teachers.

The University you prophet.

Library is very important. Bordered and shops.

Department Store and restaurants.

Here bozichka, the drink, so satisfyingly smooth, the texture.

As I really liked it. Hai provide, impression.

How many small here at Spiritualized mud.

Eye thy beautiful radiation.

Here and Asya and talents.

I established Plovdiv.

Gallery!

15) The Movement- way of the existence of matter!

Exchange of substances, energy credits.

And information conveyor.

And lightning fighting with my land.

Over sectarian ground and space.

There is talk of evolution. Energy flight.

And a large explosion every hectare there Roy.

Grass, trees, ice and dinosaurs code.

And reason, an external benchmark.

Weeping, speech, and labor, and comfort.

One to the other you have the form has wiped out.

Geological repentance. First bailiff, and in bailiff ducked.

The Bible is always repeated. Here risk and land, biologically one.

China 5 as soon as possible once and for all.

Gallery!

16) Witchcraft (quantum mechanics)!

Had flashed disease is so great Danes.

Uncovered world, cholera scourge.

A very terrifying plague.

Has done horrific things.

As contacting, was Oxford.

Here scientists, how many imagined.

Grass, conspiracy, the Liberty Bell. Have Heaven.

The Russian Orthodox Church, Pauline knew.

She appealed to heaven.

How strong the bells. It is time for this to stop. Art print on canvas --- agniart.ru knew the truth.

Sheet,epos, solution.

 And parsley is good.

And lavender, as well as is saved.

Honey excellent day version has veered quite far.

Prayer and the links. Hygiene is the soul.

Much has saved. .AND "the last of Canada".

Herbs, tea, as well as were very pleased.

The Royal wise courtyard.

How many invest in Oxford.

And Sorbrn as Richelieu.

He was looking for skit in distress.

It is difficult to it was Louis Pasteur.

Next vaccines, here is an example.

Products & Services at the Church.

He studied trail path.

Then there are also map units.

With quantum you. We found books, we knew.

He was looking for at all the response.

Many knew and Avicenna.

And Noah Descendants, science value.

Religion and spontaneous.

How much experience, and was able to.

Two ways to come together.

How many, many forces.

Gallery!

17) Rabbit Hole !

No doubt , the point of Planck .

Abundant not alone.

All the energy is full .

You unconditional goodness.

In the universe, dimensionally .

I wave envelops, the Earth , yes.

 Simultaneously.

In the past, the future, today.

And in the fourth dimension .

There is some glow .

Then at the junction after death.

Not known for certain.

There is what that way with us.

Now the Galaxy .

Transformation, transition.

Well, what awaits us there?

This is the law of attraction.

He was always in love with you.

Galileo, Copernicus, Newton.

How much knowledge in all science.

You try you, Harvey.

You create your own Coliseum.

Avicenna, Paracelsus.

Medicine is all there is.

Only physics given.

Understand how and what.

Gallery!

18) A Hopkins is not true weirdo!

We read Dr. Maikal so.

He meditsinoi valued.

Identic in University humid.

Gallery!

19) I believe will benefit! (Genetics)!

Iceland, Iceland.

There, have blood banks.

Genetics, genetics.

You want to read them all.

It is stored in the ice.

Scientists come in handy.

Make, life safer.

And better and more beautiful.

That we all carry in the blood?

Disease all is harsh.

Why do we love the mountains?

We love all the spaces.

What is biochemistry?

As important destiny.

What prospects?

And what prerogatives?

How often donate blood?

And what prevented it?

How to eat?

Who married and combined?

Should be repeated stubbornly.

Nature, she does not get tired.

And medicine support.

Lord, I believe.

Keep it up.

Gallery!

20) Cir. Raw !

Ah Tze very raw venerated.

Age long you kept.

You are wise, crafty, sweet.

Very feminine, happy.

While it won.

Etiquette you learned.

Art and a lot of flying.

People respected you.

Know the customs of their fathers.

Diplomats, merchants.

Beautiful geisha terrible secrets.

You are the ruler.

What is the gift?

You were friends with makeup.

Fashion you idolized.

Only time, that's fate.

On the pages you are always.

Anticipate that you could?

What is your logic?

Why power is important?

You stayed, by her.

What has kept you for so long?

It's just you, could.

That providence case.

Maybe it's too old.

Is it objective?

Gallery!

21) Review!

Review, review.

You're not static.

Sometimes because you're critical.

And I'm a student.

Give assessment and analysis.

Scheme and have space.

How do I get to your reception?

Long, you exist?

And the world you alter.

You exacerbate hearing and sight.

You appreciate the taste and outlook.

You supply and demand.

Always you direction.

Some caress and eat.

And we're to maieutic.

You always theatrical.

More verbal notes.

Gallery!

22) Taoist monks in America!

People always blow.

Ancestral experience, studying.

He is akin to the universe, so.

The world is looking for what he is?

Learn the state.

Changes consciousness.

Experience falcon.

Confucius style.

Aikido protection spire.

That's America East.

How common is expensive.

Then Elena Blavatsky.

Extends Eykumenu.

How many monasteries?

How many teachers?

Great, smart Statutes.

Century 13 Gaudeamus.

As scientists combine.

How can strengthen our spirit.

Information because squalls.

And remember they are not enough.

Gallery!

23) Yes force is with you!

Remember Plovdiv and Sorbon .

There was a doctor; he's in love with life.

He is a wonderful therapist.

And everywhere a great success.

And his wife is sick.

And in a wheelchair.

Sclerosis, as it struck.

Peace, did not win.

And now there is hope too.

Myelin, sounds like gently.

How many tears, prayers and requests.

We believe in this post.

What a marriage, what a saint?

Why is he responsible?

How difficult it is to survive.

If there is no hurry.

And I always believe in the power.

If anything, so I asked.

And I asked more than once.

You saved the world for us.

Was in intensive care.

Mother asked me.

Ashgabat, Semashko froze.

Well all of you, I begged.

Gallery!

24) In a glass of wine should be drunk!

Heike tenderness is born.

All shades, lotus colors.

This world is all the lights.

In light of a poet.

Observation, experience, and paints.

And the comparison of the puzzle.

Mind that it already knows.

A poet dreams about?

World of the poet is very complicated.

He knows everything in advance.

Since childhood, happy, affectionate it.

Omar Khayyam, he riddles.

Gallery!

25) Jewish humor!

Today is the day, today is the moment.

Israel creates poetry.

Soul of happiness lit.

Shalom Aleichem said.

He humor so adores.

Points it out because he was not wearing a Rabi.

Frame window itself to the world.

That's better than nothing so.

First one tooth ached.

Then another very **dumb**.

Then suddenly, he becomes ill.

But it's better than what else.

Rabbi suddenly read prayers.

About grandchildren he remembered.

What is this?

One in Odessa and one in Tel Aviv.

Toothache he suddenly forgot.

Gallery!

26) Trail!

Look there is a trail it is steep.

Oh, it's golden grove.

Violets clarity burn.

How lovely is the leaf.

Purple blue of the molds.

We are impressed, splendor.

There's barely a trickle murmurs.

Listen thrush, what it says.

Like a waterfall in the distance shines.

What if Amazon grumbles?

Woods and luxurious become dark.

And we are with you, and no guilt.

There, there is a very long bridge , then Sofia.

Poles giant glove.

I Gaidar you read.

I remembered a long time.

Now I do not remember ever.

Why we went there.

But who has dreamed about it?

About it, I did not forget.

Sounds great, to me in triumph.

I sing live, love destiny.

Gallery

27) Beowulf!

Denmark, Denmark, a piece of the universe!

Legends come from antiquity.

Epic message, all knows them.

There's life, and describe warriors heard.

There's a strong character, full of courage those.

Fought for the expulsion, monsters and country.

Princess in expectations, they, too, went into battle.

Heroes are remarkable, full of determination.

Not just competition, victory came to them.

But the wounds are fatal, because dragons are tricky.

And the ocean water they save, not helped.

Dragons defeated all the people released.

But Beowulf buried you, you burned bonfires.

About memory and tradition, they are still alive.

Gallery!

28) Savants!

Conventional wisdom, Very simply instantly!

Only private, it is!

Unknown, new!

World care about autism!

Their solution, as artists!

And fantasy flight!

Suddenly, to discoveries leads!

Private, honestly, as a sudden!

Extends hands brain!

Particularly through lead!

And provide solutions!

Positive disease cures!

Gene changes!

In inflammation breakdown!

You are now completely different!

Gallery!

29) Ludwig Guttman ! (Neurosurgeon)!

I catch any bit.

I see a large retinue.

Not staggered, fell.

Illness is not broke.

Ludwig Guttmann, a neurosurgeon.

He invented the sport and leisure.

He made the Olympics.

For patients at large, enjoy.

And raised their children there.

Wheelchair, Learn to see everything.

Invalid does not mean coward.

Master, Learn to see, the record shall stone.

Orthopedics developed.

Playfulness is very handy.

Learn to see you on the prosthesis.

Meet the game, get over.

Gallery!

30) Amok!

Amok work.

Here Zweig wonders.

The tutorial is found.

And life is in trouble.

Medicine echoes.

From literature sometimes.

A novel of life is the link.

In art and everything related.

And Chekhov, Giotto in the world window.

Philosopher Maimonides, so instituted.

Conflicts should be avoided.

And Hume, Freud knows better.

In Africa, there is, in the novel.

Thrilling plot.

As loyalty economized.

Because doctors give a oath.

Gallery!

31) Emergency Water! (Australia)!

In Australia, there is such a service.

As citizens living on the water, to save?

How long are the train, they and their path.

Years compete Miléai that dream.

What exercises and everywhere there is jerk.

With gymnastics are fighting to overcome the wave.

How to make faster?

How to become someone even stronger?

In any weather.

And even a severe storm.

Those jump in the water.

To save your life.

Calm, very cute.

You lie down on the sand.

Gallery!

32) Theatre and Dance!

Italian comedy in Paris.

Masque and Piero .

Jesters, it really opened.

Gaby and white, what's this?

Here Harlequin costume, rags.

There's jacket and pants.

And the mask with a long beard.

Crispin servant, and he is a hero.

Dancer Camargo.

And floss, which is very important.

Spanish captain.

There Scaramouche , Tartaglia .

This clan.

Gallery!

33) Porcelain figurines!

Rococo, you're very sweet.

Form shells motif.

" Dancer ", " Group cowherd."

"Dancer", here's an overview.

Grace motive.

Porcelain aristocratic embodied.

Miniature, very kind.

Nature, graceful face.

Waking perfect he used.

Gallery!

34) How to drive a car!

Two neurons synapse are there.

Electricity is tidings.

If that connection again.

That foothold in consciousness.

Pleasure signal.

Support imperial.

The more pleasurable emotions.

Those need to communicate, promotion.

Associations swarm.

Entail consciousness behind.

7 icons are stored.

This strengthens memory.

What would consolidate stronger?

More knowledge to invest there.

Come up with a variety of scenes.

Very colorful and important.

Compositions are not simple.

Links delicate, gold.

Fear gives us the memory too.

We remember that it is not unseemly.

Give a clue, because the sign must.

Make a careful knowledge.

Deceive beautiful brain.

And to make an important knowledge flesh.

Extreme situations.

Gives us the coronation.

Fancy them.

So to build bridges.

Temperament, expressiveness.

Can give and aggressiveness.

Those remembered faster.

Surprise those people.

How to strengthen the same memory?

Necessary with something to fix.

Gallery!

35) Laugh Clown over a broken love!

Italian soul.

Verdi, Rigoletto " jester ".

Forgot the words to tra la la .

Tenor sang spark grief.

And in " Othello " by Rossini.

Gold you baptized.

Hall wept inspiration.

How cute is the moment?

"Tosca" passport at home he forgot.

The bank received the money.

He sang the aria tried.

And he waited for the loan.

Gallery!

36) El Greco!

Free confidence.

Manners and letters.

And strange eternal.

She was always full.

A very special view of the world.

And this mentality, idol.

Here composition is bold.

And it seems like surprised.

Here all forms, curved.

Here unusual strokes.

Portraits " inner soul."

Those unusual and bold.

And what that background is not so.

Well, in general it is a connoisseur large.

He loved, very humanists.

Moralists and philosophers.

All historical husbands.

Among them are many kings.

Gallery!

37) Scottish highlanders!

As Homer's " Iliad."

That song for mountaineers' courage.

World stories in joy.

After all accounts and so not enough.

As protected memory.

And pipers saved.

From all clans knew well.

By Douglas, June, armor noise.

Warrior Clan Kvoriez.

To win the crown.

Piper of Clan Krumin .

Spirit inspired his comrades.

Plaid of Clan Sinclair.

He is now convenient to all.

Kennedy clan store.

Men now wear a kilt.

Women are the kind he apron.

He is defender, has cells of a godson.

Gallery!

38) Poetry Israel!

Here you poetry Israel.

Dobrzyński represents.

You're serious, because of Adam.

Have talents, the path they are given.

You Themis warmed.

How many times have sung.

Through difficulties to success.

As we strive for it?

Get everything right.

You are responsible, with taste, tone.

Interesting circle of friends.

Architects, doctors.

In medicine, he is well versed.

In love with TV.

Always busy, on business.

But in poetry you can't .

Gallery!

39) " Top down the stairs!"

In the synagogue, the synagogue.

Concert Klyayzerov, as much.

Very good violin.

That thoughtful, cheerful.

How much humor, stories?

Very fun wedding.

Violin lost peace.

For my soul, king.

Maybe somewhere Rabinovich?

He will tell you what is the news?

He lives in America.

And the ink, no longer pours.

Who is " up and down the stairs is?"

This granddaughter, she teaches.

Who approved the awards?

For a world of talent.

Only beauty will save the world.

And talents, as a calling.

Gallery!

40) Ducky, how beautiful your saga!

Burebista and Decebalus!

Ducky of Thracian, tribes you.

And you Danube family, home.

Rome was not time, you won.

And defended, freedom .

Know of wool, wears hats.

Women work, love of courage.

Difficult, long, was either way.

How much courage and work.

Tempered youth.

Trained to fight in a ford.

How dare was the same people.

It was in the nature of the wolf.

Initiation rite.

How much loyalty, all in harmony.

Hands placed on a tree stump.

Not hurt their blade.

Body could feel.

Your strong sons.

How beautiful is the queen.

You managed to raise sons.

We are eager, recognition.

On Earth, let there be peace.

Bucharest, he was in full bloom.

I love the colors of life.

Loves opera, theater.

There is also universal holiness.

Gallery!

41) And Unilyuks peruarki !

Unilyuks and peruarki .

Not alone here but beams.

How many windows here.

Here platform and fox.

Information blocks here.

Furniture, appliances, roads.

Here various plastics.

Fancy terraces.

Spa and sauna all deluxe.

That pool, olive bush .

How many stairs and walkways.

Stained glass windows, balconies, intercoms.

Ceilings for design.

This house you colonize.

8 rooms, floors.

How many windows and doors?

Lift, cellar and garage.

Sadik , grandmother , all of us .

That's what water.

Heating comfort.

On top of a greenhouse.

Boiler type Prometheus.

On the upside, as the king.

And his beautiful wife.

Bathsheba course not.

But it is very interesting.

Slim waist, okay figure.

And the kids and all, nature .

They look like his father.

And too pushy.

And then honor the animal.

Company wise, let him live.

Gallery!

42) Neuroscientist Jill!

Jill fine performance.

You're a professor, you have the ability.

How is a complex brain?

And about the functions, then post.

Right together, left apart.

Left sees everything in pictures.

Right in the characters lives.

And chirps and sings.

Right through all of us together.

With the subtle world and idol.

And Nirvana is given to us.

It protects us.

Left past stores.

Right to the future silent.

Subconscious and order.

All stores that we have been given.

Because yoga does not live in vain.

She relaxes .

Alpha , beta radiation.

State - saving .

Jill science connect.

With the right that has always been friends.

Could be abstracted.

No stroke medicine you saved.

Not everything is given to know before.

Lord we still care.

For that and knowledge gives.

Who knows he will not lose.

Forewarned is protected.

Obtained experience and fathers.

It protects against tricky and enemies.

And intuition is home.

Gallery!

43) Sobbed breath 1:3 !

Sobbing breath, giving love!

Tzu passionate eruption!

Rejuvenating again!

Erasing all wrinkles!

Absolutely no gray!

Health returns!

Now turn on you!

You've become a mania for us!

A disease there is no way!

Gallery!

44) The rainy season!

Sun hid recently.

Not see its rays.

Become wet, very wet.

The rainy season.

How exactly wills it last?

Who do not know any?

Immediately it was so wonderful.

And fine and light.

The sun will soon smile.

And continue to cover.

Goodbye heavy.

It will be warm again.

Fira Zavyalova .

45) Dalmatic!

800 grand a year.

Charlemagne, God's race.

According to legend, the monastery introduced dalmatic.

Vatican and Rome ruler.

Gold and precious stones.

Woven scenes masters there.

And Louis lord.

World of Art, the Louvre opened.

Then create a gallery.

And salons assemblies.

And artists Earth.

Could make copies.

Veronese those went .

And the Vicomte de Bragelonne .

Dumas in love with him.

There's a Cote d'Azur .

Laced, steel, empiricist.

There's over a cup of Balzac coffin.

With Mrs. cute says.

About " sharpen skin " .

A love he is silent.

Couturier invented fashion.

And jabot idolizes.

Louis with his minister.

A pastel and portrait.

On the art of speaking.

Doctor for warrior's reform.

About ballet about spirits.

And on the Seine, on the run.

France is not just.

Louvre, Pasteur, Sarbon Napoleon .

As the history of love.

Notre Dame de Paris .

Save the world of art.

Gallery!

46) Smart home!

Here Feng Shui, smart home.

Here kids full swarm.

Here mattresses "Robin Hood".

Here and deck bloom.

That aquarium and Kenar .

And best of La Scala tenor.

Area here to study.

Every mathematician is seen.

Installation for the game.

Jazz drum and whales.

Here and there a string orchestra.

World without music because is cramped.

That shooting, Hollywood.

Pestalozzi and Safari here.

Picasso and Sartre.

That's what the marker here.

It has its own library.

How much knowledge of etiquette.

About costumes, about the movie.

Given about Australia.

A lot of pictures.

Because here, good luck .

Here Easter, tableware .

Carnival, Purim miracle.

Gallery!

47) Purim!

Purim joy to children!

How important news are here!

Packs, masks and small animals!

And Haman's ears!

Monkeys, lions!

Musketeer's kings!

Esther heroine here!

Imitation and example!

How much beauty is here!

All stories are important!

Upbringing, relatives!

Dad, Mom, well, I am!

Be happy small children!

Gallery!

48) David!

Michelangelo loving!

And in the shower, a carrying!

Marble suddenly took a fancy!

Finally created a masterpiece!

Each of muscle, vibrant look !

He dreams he knows you!

He vertex stories!

And so sensitive is visible!

It's all in the past and in the Past!

Of course, he's in love!

Michelangelo is a child!

How valuable are you to me!

He is a standard of beauty!

Whether in the future, he lives!

Beauty is always beckoned!

Generates gifts and orders!

And posture, fighter torso!

Will is tempered!

Gallery!

49) Hypothesis! (Past and future)!

Do pigs have intelligence?

Where would you do it?

Where is the snowman?

What is it in the future as a message?

If suddenly glaciation?

Evolution, creations.

And clouds on Mars.

Without protein path.

Who was the first giant?

Or small coral?

How to understand and how to come up?

Who? Are they all the same, the first live?

After Tsiolkovsky who else knew?

Maybe future ball?

Why suddenly cosmists?

BCO universe settled?

How, then, we suddenly understand?

Why the engine again?

Cities need to be there.

It is very important module you.

Need very beliefs.

Knowledge of new solutions.

What is it, the Ocean?

What's going on in there?

As the Galaxy and the Sun?

You cannot delete.

How to expand our consciousness?

And rapid method for reading?

Was that the ancient man?

Awareness, than our age?

Why jellyfish and dolphins?

So understood, the reasons?

And in China, the place is.

To 130 and their countless.

Young people have always forward.

Well, in the past, who lives?

After Descartes wrote back.

" Knowledge is power " is a fact.

La Mettrie was still dreaming.

People all over the world has known.

As luck would have to beg?

And the protection and forgiveness?

Gallery!

50) Painting of the world!

Hospice, hospice.

One way.

In the world of the mind.

What moved?

Sky, air and water.

Mythology always.

I am a child in the universe.

What's behind the door, I need?

Accumulation, explosion, jump.

I'm in the future connoisseur.

I am a seeker and a fighter.

But always with you creator.

I go back, not the end.

Gallery!

51) Eduard Monet!

He often visited the Louvre.

There he rented copies.

Certainly loved Titian.

Rembrandt and " Judith ".

He wrote " Boy with a dog."

And a series of still lives.

They are so bright, rainbow burn.

" Beautiful is breakfast on the grass."

And "Olympic" he price.

Those are full composition.

Flowers, fruit slim.

Individuality he loved.

By contrast, velvet struck.

Oh, peach! How beautiful.

And grapes and wrapped it.

Eels and pike.

Oysters and lemon.

Those shade semitone .

Beautiful bun in the " brioche ".

And very pleasant rosette.

Gallery!

52) Siamese twins !

Mother said : " The book is."

On the fate of her reading.

There's great things.

Let the one true way.

Carlos read much so.

And he knew the art.

As it is difficult to write an essay?

Because the word, then the satellite God.

Mathematics, law.

Well, physics, protons?

Mendel important, or not?

And spirituality, poet .

His credo in the dispute took.

And brain activity intensity.

How many were there teams.

As a result, the threshold is taken.

How complicated anesthesia .

How can your heart? In the rhythm of beating?

Nevertheless became a pediatrician .

He delighted all moms.

Established a prestigious fund.

To know the tone.

Are there many evils?

Win in the blink of an eye?

Blue, pink gene?

As mysteriously complicated?

Coarctation laws.

Man, what did he?

Gallery!

53) The Golden Hour!

First hour.

He, gold.

Best Center.

In Miami it is.

It employs spices.

With a shock they are fighting.

A system.

Epinephrine and dopamine.

And adrenaline.

Diagnosis idol.

Here you roentgen sentence.

It opens the space.

Blood will order immediately.

In the transplant will not be denied.

Honestly know algorithms.

Restore rhythms.

Podiatrist and pulmonologist.

Lab technician and resuscitator.

Those with science always.

Looking for new business.

All procedures will apply.

And he measured a criterion.

They really need a psychologist.

Lifetime, it is expensive around.

Here are important designers.

Sutures are wonderful, all on you.

Ventilator and all that breathe.

Pharmacologist also looking for.

Gallery!

54) Freud's Couch!

Couch Freud pedestal.

Always endorses.

He spoke very thinly.

Only gently closing the shutter.

He asked questions.

Memory took always full.

He discovered the laws of those.

" I did it " for which he in trouble?

What role experiences?

Why those memories?

That clothing is not easy.

Determines the sex of it.

What hormones do not sow.

And the experience of flirting.

Associations, example.

Live and in language, froze.

Carnegie also taught us.

Be able to inspire you idol.

And only the first vision.

Gives an idea of the person .

Gallery!

55) The Brazilian tango forever!

Fashion, fashion you JNA.

Very vital.

Raises sails.

SOCIAL road.

Develop a better taste.

Rejuvenates. Ace.

Wellbeing gives.

You and creed eternal institution.

You posture straightens.

Kilograms you slow down.

Philosophize calling.

Grammy, Oscar is growth.

You reap what you sow.

If you see gray.

So fashionable she is.

Facial wrinkle.

Here cosmetics hitch.

Eternal hat with fields.

Well, because handbag with us.

Diamonds are not saved.

If there is no great achievements.

Well-being is important.

How many grandchildren here it is.

"Body language" I read.

In the mirror I know myself.

I say 17.

I teach well, you.

Lesson sweet, affair.

You become a millionaire.

Youth is very good.

Well, because maturity is important.

90 are not a crime.

And 120 are given in proc.

And well, there you fashion.

Try us to believe.

Mikvah because your soul.

Never gets old.

Brazilian tango that.

Gallery!

56) Bosch!

He had the courage.

Show the world from the inside.

And the name of a point of pride.

Hieronymus Bosch lightface.

"Garden of Delights" seems.

His self-portrait.

And so very mysterious.

Image " Banquet".

It is known that the "Crucifixion".

Ceremony " Marriage at Cana ".

And the eternal knowledge.

Calvary and Christ.

" Ship of Fools."

Satire he was born.

Characters and obsessions.

And a plurality of confessions.

Gallery!

57) Francis Bacon!

Big nose.

He is scientist clockwork.

" Atlantis " he taught.

" New " he baptized her.

How many of his idols.

You have not forgotten about that.

They say he is an engineer.

The best example of the art.

Why not forgotten?

The engine belongs to him?

Space he knew.

Ocean he was saying.

Social structure.

Requires partnership forever.

He was fond of the idea.

Before the new without timidity.

He was a partner of science.

That theater, 100 caves.

How was space?

Idol of all his failed.

He liked to experiment.

Where is the philosopher, there present .

Gallery!

58) That fluoresces!

Two ways and two starters.

That's what the maxim.

Eva possible with children held here.

How many guesses, the first mother is she?

Antiquities cute destiny sentence.

Neanderthal you so bold.

And he also removed the Cro-Magnon.

Between them the starting point.

Sea of hope and friendship.

Here all events, given by God.

This development, the world fauna.

And bathyscaphe idol for all of us.

You on a tour? Strangely.

Eilat is the world represented.

How many beaches, warmth and comfort.

Relationship with Israel.

It awaits guests.

Gallery!

59) Bacchus and Ariadne!

Titian loved Goddesses.

Favianov and satyrs.

Mythology is a school.

Because he was the foundation.

Landscapes and portraits.

And glorified subjects.

Venice, son always.

Yes surprising approach.

His analysis of the senses.

And the splendor of the music.

The compositions and paints.

He loved so carelessly.

Very nervous brushstrokes.

Expressive and free.

As they are saturated.

And full of harmonies.

Ariadne daughter of the king of Crete.

In love God Bacchus.

Feeling so quickly arose.

Dazzling and clean.

The sky suddenly hoisted the crown.

He lit constellation.

She burned immortality.

Gods blessed marriage.

Chariot harnessed.

Since she cheetahs.

Very pink cape.

Cobalt cute bird.

Light clothing suits her.

He suddenly spawned a wave.

Cobalt struck Bacchus.

And smile flashed.

Gallery!

60) Before Science!

Suddenly came the great glacier.

Cold in the house is slightly infiltrated.

There is no longer trees, grasses.

Harvested him.

Mineral water.

Even in the cold hot.

That saved and from his wounds.

Subcutaneous layer overgrown.

Full pleasure.

This seems to be like a spa.

Collected under roots here.

Fruits collected in winter.

Salt and learned about the cold.

Understand what he is young.

Clay, twigs, plaster bandage.

Rubbing and massage.

Protects you forever.

Chiropractor became honorary.

But he removed the tooth.

Birth to the child 's mother.

As we swaddle him.

If there is a temperature.

Pupovinka, back, breast.

Well, of course wine.

And rescued it.

Born knowing so.

In before science at the time.

Astronomy and numbers count.

Philosophies honor.

There is a legend in the world came from.

Eykumenu found.

Intuition saved.

Bravery strongly rescued.

Experience, knowledge, honor.

The elderly already have side.

Sorcerers and Pahari .

Fishing and hunting.

Medicine here's quota.

Gallery!

61) Retro, how?

Batak so many streets.

And as retro? So I felt sad.

Soon winter will not go.

Church of the past leads.

How many here snowdrifts.

In the eye of the sun is not included.

A spark from the pipe knocks.

The house has great food.

Still, like pickles.

Bluberries, everything in fashion.

And of course there is the wine.

Domadzhany , children -in-law .

It's so soft, so warm.

As a light frost.

Bread on the tablecloth lies.

And an appetizer says.

" Temple" love is all knit.

And " Bojur " tells about the handbag.

" Nikerman " lies in the corner.

" And our house" design creates.

Very old clock.

After all, they are Swiss.

Samotkal all flowers.

Cerga 's circle and you.

Gallery!

62) Dance Class! (Psychology Dance)!

Degas ballet so adored.

And filigree sang.

He admired the bright sash.

He emphasized his spot.

In "Grand Opera" it was his.

Photographed loved.

He sketched system dexterous feet.

And the rhythm and grace, so what?

Terrier and watering near the feet.

That eye for what that could catch on.

Retrospective showed.

That lens sculpture created us.

Worked more in the studio.

Theo lost peace.

Painting he sold at auction.

Last year.

He gave her French.

Gallery!

63) A double portrait! (Jan van Eyck)!

Arnolfini are couple.

Not sunk into the abyss.

That hung in the kitchen.

Not valid.

Today is very important.

There, all always gracefully.

Lovely Couple.

Fragment she entered.

Here olives paint.

Chains like a mask.

Wife in a green and heavenly.

Palm trusting and snow.

The rite was held too.

And he was married in the church.

And at the helm of the mirror.

Their silhouettes floated.

And the little dog.

Allowed to remain.

At the moment he is very passionate.

Let enjoy.

Well that all couple parted.

Only after she left.

And we are all waiting for a decision.

Some glow.

Gallery!

64) Healthy Eating!

Healthy food.

How important is for us.

Then we formation.

And sports need an hour.

French love wine.

And the Italians that?

That's how it invented.

120 as it are?

What sort of calories?

What is there to fats?

And as we have cholesterol.

Try supported.

We like very much the fish.

Forshmak we love.

We can no longer roast.

Not salty.

Mush yet.

And toast to nothing.

And if you want a cake.

Napoleon buy.

We algae sweet.

Calories , that's what .

Taste apples are not forgotten.

And make friends with pears.

Cabbage has beneficial.

Fiber because there is.

All soy too.

A buckwheat why?

Vitamins around us.

How many oranges.

I love avocados.

How glad Okinawa.

Not devoid of movement.

Always something to their liking.

Another Blessing.

I 'm friends with Toroyu .

Gallery!

65) Cinquecento !

Leonardo, Raphael, Michelangelo.

Shape, tone, pastel.

Fighting spirit, talents battle.

Titian wise dispute.

Perugino student.

Previous talent not wilted.

He is a singer flickering light.

And he worked until dawn.

Knew the laws of perspective.

Anatomy landscape.

Chiaroscuro strong rush.

Vanguard, all on display.

Stanza dello Senyatura.

Decorated arch shape.

Murals, stations all from nature.

This is a " Dispute" is not simple.

Show all , Biblical argument.

Theology Communion dispute.

Very prominent fathers.

Transcendental philosophy was.

It reflects the world.

Poetry red, virtuous, modest.

Legal law.

Raphael Madonnas.

Fornarina standard.

Gallery!

66) Contrast and perception!

Still loved Van Gogh.

He was in Paris and everywhere.

And learned those laws.

In colors, the sky , at the rink.

He explored the palette.

Was familiar with the theory and rhythm.

"The Bible " and " dear friend."

Those decorated leisure.

Clear vertical reef.

Subordination , he penetrated .

Navy blue light flare.

It was his picnic.

The similarity of spirit and fighting spirit.

Red.

He quite quiet.

Iris took quite wilted.

Purple, violet.

It contrasts, very new.

He is fine, not great,

Look closely, because all of it is yours.

Gallery!

67) Lao Tzu!

Tao, Taoism.

In all things through.

Form, sign the measure blast.

All knowledge in a mess.

Yin and Yang so where the beginning?

Mid any.

That end, where the creator of the heavenly forces ?

Writing nature healing.

And verses heat creation.

All laws unravel.

Learn to understand everything.

Become flush with the universe.

Anger take yes curb.

All the secrets we know.

How to recognize the language of birds?

Gallery!

68) Guernica! (Pablo Picasso) !

Known creation.

Eternal love.

Guernica unforgettable.

It 's your child.

And cherished memory.

You are in the genes canvas.

Such atrocities.

They cannot live again.

We like that they bind together.

Divine circle.

We all have a duty as that.

Yad Vashem avoid.

We have one ancestral home.

Single eternal way.

Let us love the motherland.

And the world will always keep.

Picasso, Chagall and Munch.

Matisse, Courbet and La Kurbat.

Cubism, Modernism, Impressionism .

How many worthy visas.

Gallery!

69) Sirtaki ! (Or ours!)

Oh Sirtaki you fire!

Very groovy dance!

The stones on the road!

You led all for yourself!

Here Sirtaki , the Horo !

As we like it!

Musician fur puffed out!

Feet, legs, help!

A costums their colors!

Drums beauty!

How much pace and enthusiasm!

I Cathedral in love!

Gallery!

70) Peripatetic!

In the garden, walked slowly.

And they said, barely breathing.

A " form " contents ideas.

And before the teacher intimidated.

And knowable miles soul.

And how great is the measure.

Why do we need logic.

A method once and for all.

And the debate, " dialogue."

Tell me what it was prologue.

What is the universe?

And there, our destiny?

Why it took you?

And since then has it been?

Plato's " The Republic" why?

Has every star.

Socrates, Plato and Aristotle.

Hegel, Kant argues those very much.

Tell me, but what do they hurt?

Know yourself, move nature.

And in the past was striving.

Anticipate future decision.

And what is life and death?

And that person knows?

Gallery!

71) Respecting a little man!

If you look in the mirror.

There is much to see.

Even in ancient times gibbon.

Face and knew about it.

Reflection of the soul.

All emotions visible.

Passion and tenderness affect.

Dulled the pain and grief.

To see the child in it.

Time to relax and unwind.

Regard the fact, heal.

And inspire confidence.

That will take all by yourself.

I see the individual.

Reflection savage.

That natural path.

And Alice in Wonderland.

This is Carroll's dreams.

Stories, tales expectations.

With justice trys .

Gallery!

72) Red, blue, green!

Delacroix, romantic ardor.

By what stage composed.

Now the world will hear about the explosion.

And bullet terrible hunter lion suddenly won.

How restless horse, furious.

Headlong rush off he is read.

Nature is not too gentle.

Kill not tolerate, because it.

Not climax moment.

And only the previous century.

Now here's a shot sounds.

And the blood of the Earth tinge.

He all the nerves.

And in the heat.

Hunter, lion defends whether his own life?

Comes from wood wave.

Nature is so full of passion.

And even twenty years later.

She was not cold.

And the experience is complete.

You're done Delacroix.

Gallery!

73) Ora in the woods! (Fourth paragraph)!

With mom 's hand goes.

Acquaintances to know.

Eucalyptus trees stand in a row.

Ora knows her outfit.

Oranges, tangerines .

Very tasty vitamins.

Sun looks from above.

That's like a cloud.

Oh dogs here.

All friends.

And not hurt none.

Because they need training.

That carries a rubber.

And another and cart.

There Ralfushka passed.

Doesn bypassed.

He looks with high.

That's supposedly a good soul.

Well, Levick , one minister .

Ralph is always running after him.

Boris loves so picturesquely.

Stroll dogs sedately.

Ora is not afraid of them.

And a tree rushes.

That's not a lion and a bird.

Lori bow runs.

And for you as follows.

Tail waving.

It repels flies.

All past, all looked.

And with each other smiling.

Oh good walk.

Ora mom is not alone.

There is such a conglomerate.

Each meeting was so pleased.

Rally raced past us.

Hour walk with no end.

Gallery!

74) Aura in the garden. (Third part) !

Ora goes to kindergarten.

The second year in a row already.

There toys row to row.

Zebra , ostrich , giraffe.

Barbie doll rover.

And of course a cute cat.

There lies the puzzle decorum.

From this kind of composition.

You podramku gather.

That's the art of the full stroke.

Analyst and idol.

You glorified all over the world.

Many books in Hebrew.

And English is not offended.

That's where soft toys.

All age are sitting.

The entire scheme is not silent.

And naughty boys.

A golden braids.

Ora knows gamut too.

And movements are smooth, similar.

Sport, dance.

Inflated ball game here.

Knows how to raise the shoulder.

Foot stomp, defend.

That swings, slides code.

This breathtaking set.

There and skiing on the go.

I did not fall with them.

Educators smart.

Speech therapists and spices.

Ora growing bold.

Bypass all the boys.

Ora says something.

And gives emotions.

That is about to speak.

Intelligence that glitters.

Gallery!

75) Hanukkah and Ora!

Hanukkah we go.

Ora mother garden awaits.

Leggings with lace.

Dress with bows.

New shoes.

Such as in Sarochka.

In backpack toys.

Giraffe it on the pillow.

Those waiting for the bus together.

For children it is given.

Garden all decorated.

Became a favorite, our.

Dance, music, parade.

Candles burn brightly there.

About the past they say.

Give a lot of joy.

Here balloons and flags.

How much courage in them.

Triumph round boils.

Israel gives them childhood.

Gallery!

76) Ora and Zebra!

Ora mom.

Safari looks.

Feeding the birds out of the car.

Buy volenochek away.

He shies ahead.

Mother yells: you do not go .

Ora very good.

Right kind soul.

Cine chirps.

Kangaroo screen laughing.

And also wants goodies.

Galka on the back of a hippopotamus.

No in her care.

In a pond all in a row.

Somewhere near a waterfall.

Burning rays of him.

Ora in cap sits.

The sun is shining haze hovers.

That tired no power.

Gallery!

ABOUT THE AUTHOR

Iliyan Yurukov graduated from the university in Ashkhabad, he is children's pediatrician.

Nellya Yurukov graduated from the university in Ashkhabad, specializing in History and Philosophy. Her hobbies are photo, design, esoteric and music. "Diviz Per aspera ad Astra" is our pseudonym, which translated in English means, "Gallery's love to France."